Full STEAM Ahead!

Arts in Action

Making Art from Anything

Robin Johnson

CRABTREE
PUBLISHING COMPANY
WWW.CRABTREEBOOKS.COM

Title-Specific Learning Objectives:

Readers will:

- Ask and answer questions about the materials used in different types of art.
- Identify different types of art and some natural and human-made materials artists use.
- Describe how artists create art by using materials in new ways.

High-frequency words (grade one) and, can, is, it, make, they, this, to, use	Academic vocabulary instruments, Inuit, mosaic, nature, quilt

Before, During, and After Reading Prompts:

Activate Prior Knowledge and Make Predictions:

Have children read the title and look at the cover images. Ask:

- What do you think the book will be about?
- What materials have you used to make art?

During Reading:

After reading pages 18 and 19, ask children:

- Why is it a good idea to make art from trash? (Encourage children to think about reusing materials as a way of helping the environment.)

- Ask children to look closely at the pictures on pages 18 and 19. What types of trash items were reused? Make a list of the items they find.
- Encourage children to make text-to-self connections by asking them if they have ever reused materials that were thrown away.

After Reading:

Make a chart of natural and human-made materials mentioned in the book. Take a walk around the school, then the playground. Ask children to be art detectives and find other materials that they think art could be made from. Add their new ideas to the chart.

Author: Robin Johnson

Series Development: Reagan Miller

Editor: Janine Deschenes

Proofreader: Melissa Boyce

STEAM Notes for Educators: Janine Deschenes

Guided Reading Leveling: Publishing Solutions Group

Cover, Interior Design, and Prepress: Samara Parent

Photo research: Robin Johnson and Samara Parent

Production coordinator: Katherine Berti

Photographs:
Alamy: Andrew Cribb: p. 11 (bottom)
Getty images: Fairfax Media: p. 21 (top)
iStock: Richard Lewisohn: p. 4
Shutterstock: Philip Lange: title page; Hang Dinh: p. 5 (top);
    Giusparta: p. 7 (top); PhotoChur: p. 7 (bottom), p. 13, p. 18;
    Bob C: p. 9 (top); EA Given: p. 10; peacefoo: p. 11 (top); Harry
    studio: p. 15 (bottom); Leonard Zhukovsky: p. 17 (bottom);
    Jillian Cain Photography; pim pic: p. 19; A. Einsiedler: p. 20,
    p. 21 (bottom)
All other photographs by Shutterstock

Library and Archives Canada Cataloguing in Publication

Johnson, Robin (Robin R.), author
        Making art from anything / Robin Johnson.

(Full STEAM ahead!)
Includes index.
Issued in print and electronic formats.
ISBN 978-0-7787-6229-4 (hardcover).--
ISBN 978-0-7787-6290-4 (softcover).--ISBN 978-1-4271-2268-1 (HTML)

        1. Found objects (Art)--Juvenile literature. 2. Refuse as art
material--Juvenile literature. 3. Handicraft--Juvenile literature. I. Title.

TT160.J64 2019   j745.58′4   C2018-906229-0
                                                        C2018-906230-4

Library of Congress Cataloging-in-Publication Data

Names: Johnson, Robin (Robin R.), author.
Title: Making art from anything / Robin Johnson.
Description: New York : Crabtree Publishing Company, 2019. | Series:
    Full STEAM ahead! | Includes index.
Identifiers: LCCN 2018056604 (print) | LCCN 2018057514 (ebook) |
    ISBN 9781427122681 (Electronic) |
    ISBN 9780778762294 (hardcover : alk. paper) |
    ISBN 9780778762904 (pbk. : alk. paper)
Subjects: LCSH: Artists' materials--Juvenile literature.
Classification: LCC N8530 (ebook) | LCC N8530 .J64 2019 (print) |
    DDC 702.8--dc23
LC record available at https://lccn.loc.gov/2018056604

Printed in the U.S.A./042019/CG20190215

Table of Contents

Crabtree Publishing Company

www.crabtreebooks.com 1-800-387-7650

Published in Canada
Crabtree Publishing
616 Welland Ave.
St. Catharines, Ontario
L2M 5V6

Published in the United States
Crabtree Publishing
PMB 59051
350 Fifth Avenue, 59th Floor
New York, New York 10118

Published in the United Kingdom
Crabtree Publishing
Maritime House
Basin Road North, Hove
BN41 1WR

Published in Australia
Crabtree Publishing
Unit 3 – 5 Currumbin Court
Capalaba
QLD 4157

What is Art?

You see art every day. Art can be pictures, dances, and music. It is anything beautiful or interesting that people look at or listen to. Artists are the people who make art.

These artists are acting in a play. A play is art that people watch.

These artists are making music.
It is art we listen to.

This artist made a basket.
A basket is art we can
look at.

Making Art

Artists can make art from anything. They can use rocks and sticks. They can use buckets and buttons. Art made of different things is fun to look at and listen to!

buttons

An artist used colorful buttons to make this art.

An artist used snow to make this **sculpture**!

Artists used different kinds of **trash** to make these dresses.

Art from Nature

Artists can make art with things that they find in **nature**. Artists use flowers, rocks, sticks, and other parts of nature.

An artist used leaves and sticks to make this butterfly.

An artist used big sticks to make this sculpture of a horse.

The **Inuit** are a group of people from the Arctic. Some Inuit are artists who use rocks to make sculptures.

Old and New

Artists can make new art from old things.
They change how something looks.
They find new ways to use something.

An artist used old boxes to make a rainbow!

An artist used old car parts to make a sculpture of a baby cow.

An artist used old bike wheels and umbrellas to make art.

Art from Clothes

Some artists use old clothes to make art. They cut the clothes into pieces. Then they make art by joining the pieces in new ways.

An artist used pieces of old clothes to make this **quilt**.

An artist used old ties to make this bird sculpture.

Art from Food

Some artists make art from food.
They can use rice and corn.
They can use fruits and vegetables.

rice

This artist is using colorful rice to make a picture.

An artist used corn **husks** to make these dolls.

This artist is using a watermelon to make beautiful art.

watermelon

Bottles and Cans

Some artists use empty food cans and bottles to make art. They can use lids and bottle caps to make art too!

An artist used bottle caps to make an under-the-sea **mosaic**.

An artist used cans of food to make this sculpture of a tree.

An artist used empty food cans to make this animal art!

tin can

17

Art from Trash

Some artists make art from things that people throw away. Things people throw away are called trash.

An artist used plastic trash to make this picture of a man.

Artists used trash from oceans and rivers to make this sculpture of a whale.

Making Music

Some artists make music with **instruments**. They can make instruments with different things.

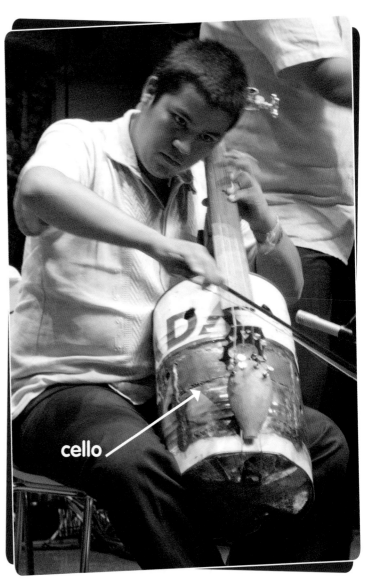

cello

This artist used a bucket to make a cello. He plays beautiful music.

These artists are using trash cans and lids to make music.

An artist used old cans to make this guitar.

Words to Know

husks [huhsks] noun
Dry shells covering
some foods

instruments [IN-struh-muh nts] noun Tools that
make musical sounds

Inuit [IN-yoo-it] noun
A group of peoples who
are from the Arctic

mosaic [moh-ZEY-ik]
noun Art made of many
small pieces

nature [NEY-cher] noun
The outside environment

quilt [kwilt] noun A
blanket made of patches

sculpture [SKUHLP-cher] noun Art made
by shaping and putting
together materials

trash [trash] noun
Things people throw
away

A noun is a person, place, or thing.

A verb is an action word that tells you what someone or something does.

An adjective is a word that tells you what something is like.

Index

About the Author

Robin Johnson is a freelance author and editor who has written more than 80 children's books. When she isn't working, Robin builds castles in the sky with her engineer husband and their two best creations—sons Jeremy and Drew.

To explore and learn more, enter the code at the Crabtree Plus website below.

www.crabtreeplus.com/fullsteamahead

Your code is:
fsa20

23

STEAM Notes for Educators

Full STEAM Ahead is a literacy series that helps readers build vocabulary, fluency, and comprehension while learning about big ideas in STEAM subjects. *Making Art from Anything* helps readers answer questions about unique art by reading about the materials from which it is made. The STEAM activity below helps readers extend the ideas in the book to build their skills in math, science, and arts.

One-of-a-Kind Mosaic

Children will be able to:
- Identify a range of natural and human-made materials from which art can be made.
- Create a mosaic using different materials.
- Create a pattern in their mosaic.

Materials
- Mosaic Planning Sheet
- Cardboard for mosaic base
- Glue
- Natural and human-made materials, such as stones, bottle caps, plastic toys, petals, etc.

Guiding Prompts
After reading *Making Art from Anything*, ask:
- What is the most interesting piece of art you read about? Why? What was it made of?

Activity Prompts
Turn to page 16 and look at the picture of a mosaic. Review the glossary definition for mosaic. Ask children:
- Why is a mosaic a good way to showcase many different materials? (As a mosaic is art made up of many small pieces put together, it's a good way to showcase many different materials put together in one piece.)

Explain to children that they will create a mosaic that showcases different materials! Their mosaic must include a pattern. Review this concept and show examples of patterns.
- Pattern: A repeated design or sequence.

Each child should fill out the Mosaic Planning Sheet. Then they will create their mosaic.

Review the criteria with children:
- Mosaic must have three or more different materials.
- Mosaic must include at least one natural and one human-made material.
- Mosaic must include a pattern.

Children can share their mosaics in small groups. They should tell peers which materials they used.

Extensions
- Have children use the same materials in a new way, to create a different type of art.

To view and download the worksheet, visit **www.crabtreebooks.com/resources/ printables** or **www.crabtreeplus.com/ fullsteamahead** and enter the code **fsa20**.